DISCOVER YOUR LIFE PURPOSE

Unleash Your True Calling,
Foster Mindful Awareness,
Attain Crystal Clear Clarity,
and Master the Art of Leading
A Meaningful Existence

Sooraj Achar

WWW.SOORAJ-ACHAR.COM

YOUR FREE GIFT

As a token of my thanks for taking out time to read my book, I would like to offer you a **Free-Gift**:

ABOUT AUTHOR

Sooraj **Achar,** the Accomplished Author of **"Discover Your Life Purpose"** - A Sensational **#1 Bestseller Across the Globe**

 Dive into the world of **Sooraj Achar**, a prodigious author hailing from Bangalore, India, whose exceptional journey is as intriguing as the profound concepts explored in his works. With **"The Ultimate Self-Healing Mastery Series,"** Sooraj has transcended borders, achieving the coveted status of **#1 Bestseller** in the United States, the United Kingdom, Canada, India, and Australia.

A Remarkable Beginnings:

Sooraj Achar's extraordinary odyssey commenced in the vibrant city of Bangalore, India. As a young dreamer, his fascination with mathematics sparked an early connection with the enigmatic world of numbers. This infatuation, initially drawn from captivating numerological stories, sowed the seeds for a lifetime dedicated to the exploration of **Numerical Mysteries**.

A Multifaceted Expert:

Today, **Sooraj Achar** stands as not just an accomplished Software Engineer but also a passionate connoisseur of **numerology** and the ancient science of **Feng-Shui (Vastu)**. His multifaceted persona extends to **coaching and consulting**, where he delves into the profound questions of Health, Relationships, Careers, and Money (HRCM). Sooraj is a certified **Ho'oponopono & EFT Healer and NLP Practitioner**, renowned for his transformative abilities in bringing about balance, harmony, and fulfillment in the lives of countless individuals.

A Seeker of Wisdom:

Sooraj's relentless quest for knowledge has led him to the intricate realms of human psychology and behavior. His dedication to understanding the human psyche and optimizing life's potential is unwavering. As a perpetual learner, he embodies the principles of optimal living and shares his wisdom to empower others to lead resourceful lives.

A Believer in Unlimited Potential:

Above all, **Sooraj Achar** is a firm believer in the limitless potential residing within each individual. He ardently champions the idea that every person possesses the capacity to achieve far beyond their self-imposed limits. Through his words and wisdom, he inspires others to unlock their hidden potential and lead lives of purpose and abundance.

For more life-altering insights, delve into Sooraj Achar's remarkable catalog of books. Visit www.sooraj-achar.com and embark on a journey of self-discovery and transformation.

Stay Connected:

Explore the latest updates, thought-provoking content, and inspiring messages from Sooraj Achar by connecting with him through our social media channels. Join us in the pursuit of a fulfilling and harmonious life.

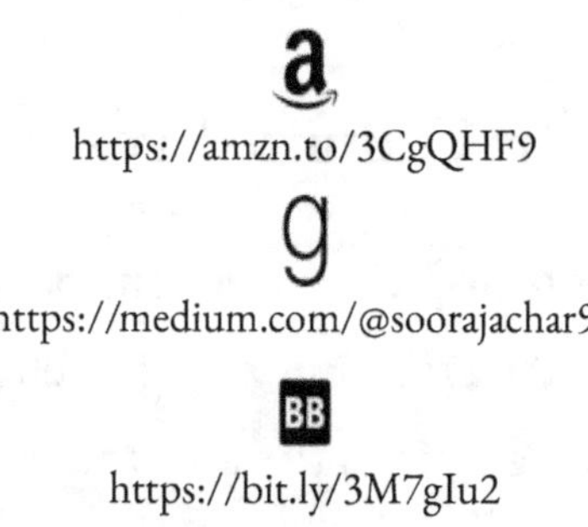

https://amzn.to/3CgQHF9

https://medium.com/@soorajachar99

https://bit.ly/3M7gIu2

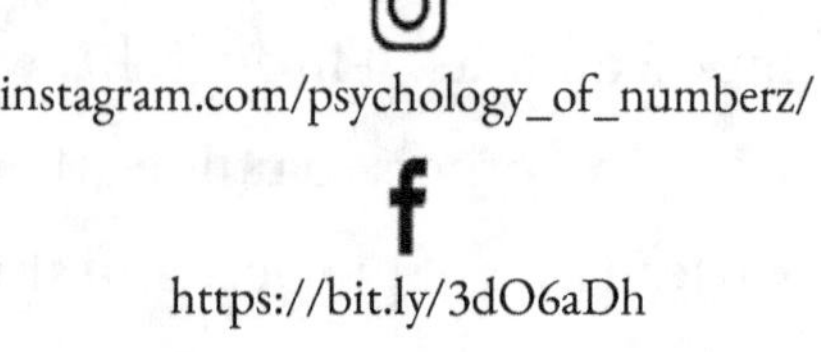

instagram.com/psychology_of_numberz/

https://bit.ly/3dO6aDh

https://bit.ly/3LXBTyz

https://bit.ly/3E9vKxc

ACKNOWLEDGEMENTS

How does a person say "**Thank You**" when there are so many people to thank?

Obviously, this book is a big thank you to my father **G Sathyanarayan Achar,** who is a powerful role model, and my mother **G Pramila,** who taught me love and kindness.

I extend my heartfelt appreciation to my sister, **Shruthi S**, brother-in-law, **Saravana P**, and adorable niece, **Naveeksha S**, who have played pivotal roles in making this book a reality. Their presence makes my life complete.

My mentor, **Mr. Mitesh Khatri**, deserves a special acknowledgment for teaching and guiding me to

become a **certified healer** in **Ho'Oponopono &
EFT** and a **NLP Practitioner**.

I owe thanks to **Mr. Som Bathla**, an **Amazon
#1 Bestselling** author, for his mentorship,
motivation, and guidance in the realms of **Writing,
Self-Publishing, and Launching Books**. His
support has been instrumental in initiating my
journey as an Authorpreneur.

Finally, heartfelt gratitude to my dedicated team –
Avesh Ansari, Akshay Bhat, and **Md. Bilal** – for
their unwavering support and contributions.

DEDICATION

This Book is Dedicated to My Grandparents,

R. Gangadhar & G. Vishalakshamma

And, My Dear Brother **Arvind Achar.**

YOUR NEXT UNFORGETTABLE ADVENTURE BEGINS HERE!

<u>Series-1</u>: <u>Master Your Life with NUMEROLOGY</u>

1. Master Your DESTINY With Numerology

2. Master Your NAME-SPELLING With Numerology

3. Master Your RELATIONSHIPS With Numerology

4. Master Your MONEY With Numerology

5. Master Your HEALTH With Numerology

6. Master Your PROFESSIONAL GOALS With Numerology

Series-2: Master Your Life with VASTU

1. Master Your DESTINY With Vastu

2. Master Your GROWTH With Vastu

3. Master Your WEALTH With Vastu

4. Master Your CAREER With Vastu

Series-3: <u>The Ultimate Self-Healing Mastery</u>

1. Discover Your Life Purpose

2. The Alchemy Of Healing

3. The Fear of Death

Series-4: Energize Your Mind, Body & Soul

1. The Art of Balancing YIN-YANG Energy

2. The 7 Energy Needs

3. The Power Of ONE Question

Series-5: LIFE-MASTERY Bundle

1. Master Your DESTINY & NAME-SPELLING With Numerology

2. Master Your HEALTH & RELATIONSHIPS With Numerology

CONTENTS

HOW THIS BOOK CAN WORK MIRACLES IN YOUR LIFE?

"Unleash the power within –
'Discover Your Life Purpose.'
Cultivate mindfulness, embrace your
passions, conquer adversities, and
let everlasting happiness be the
soundtrack of your purposeful
journey."

Embarking on a journey to discover your life's purpose is a profound exploration that can transform the very fabric of your existence. "The Magic of Discovering Life's Purpose" is not just a book; it is a guide, a beacon that can illuminate the path to your true calling.

In the labyrinth of life, finding your purpose can often feel like unraveling a mystery. This book, with its profound insights and wisdom, acts as your compass, leading you through the maze of self-discovery. The revelations within these pages are designed to work miracles in your life.

How This Book Can Work Miracles in Your Life:

1. Illuminate Your Path:

Unveil the obscured path of self-discovery and enlightenment as this book acts as a guiding light, illuminating your journey toward understanding your true calling.

2. Uncover Your True Calling:

Dive deep into the core of your being and unravel the layers that conceal your genuine life's purpose. Discover the unique and authentic calling that resonates with your soul.

3. Meaningful Existence:

This book serves as a key to deciphering the profound meaning behind your existence. It transforms the ordinary into the extraordinary, leading you to a life filled with purpose and significance.

4. Eternal Bliss Revealed:

Experience the joy of eternal bliss as you decode the secrets within. This book offers insights that can ignite a perpetual sense of happiness and contentment in your life.

5. Conquer Purposeful Living:

Equip yourself with the knowledge and revelations presented in this book to conquer the pursuit of purposeful living. Learn how to align your actions with your true calling and lead a life of fulfillment.

6. Transformative Wisdom:

The wisdom embedded in these pages has the power to work miracles by transforming your perspective on life. It provides tools and insights that empower you to shape your reality.

7. Navigate Life's Labyrinth:

Life often presents challenges and uncertainties. This book serves as your guide, helping you navigate the complexities of existence with a newfound clarity that stems from understanding your purpose.

8. Awaken Your Inner Magic:

Delve into the realms of self-awareness and awaken the magic within. This book acts as a catalyst for personal transformation, allowing you to tap into your inner reservoir of potential.

9. Create Miraculous Shifts:

By incorporating the teachings of this book, you open yourself to miraculous shifts in your life. Witness the transformative power of aligning with your true calling.

10. A Journey of Miracles:

This book is not just about reading; it's an experiential journey. Immerse yourself in the revelations it holds, and witness the miracles unfold in every aspect of your life.

"The Magic of Discovering Life's Purpose" is more than a literary work—it's a transformative experience designed to usher you into a realm of miracles, purpose, and everlasting bliss. Embrace the magic, and let the miracles unfold in your life's extraordinary tapestry.

CHAPTER HIGHLIGHTS: TOP 5 TAKEAWAYS AND INSIGHTS

1. Key Takeaways for the Chapter - In Search Of Meaning: Understanding Life's Ultimate Purpose

1. Distinguish Between Goals and Purpose: Understand the crucial difference between life goals and life purpose. Goals, such as financial success or fame, are not the purpose; rather, they are means to an emotional end.

2. Emotions Define Purpose: Realize that the true purpose of life is rooted in emotions and feelings. Every goal pursued, be it buying a house or helping others, is ultimately driven by the desire for a specific emotional experience.

3. Avoid Goal Obsession: Beware of becoming overly fixated on achieving goals at the expense of understanding and experiencing the underlying emotions that give meaning to those goals. Goal attainment without the associated emotions may lead to emptiness.

4. Individualized Emotions: Recognize that each person's purpose is unique, tied to their individual emotional needs and desires. What brings fulfillment to one person may not necessarily do the same for another.

5. Quality of Life Equals Emotions: Shift the focus from external achievements to internal experiences. The quality of life is determined by the richness of emotions and feelings experienced, emphasizing the significance of emotional fulfillment in the pursuit of life purpose.

2. Key Takeaways for the Chapter - Types Of Emotional Purposes

1. Two Emotional Life Purposes: Recognize that there are two fundamental emotional purposes in life. The first involves pursuing positive emotions like happiness, security, satisfaction, joy, and love, often linked to achieving goals such as buying a house, getting married, or acquiring material possessions.

2. Want Feelings: Understand the concept of "want feelings," where desires for luxury, recognition, and societal approval drive certain goals, like owning a luxurious car or being in a visually appealing relationship. Emphasize the importance of emotions over material achievements.

3. Marriage Emotion vs. Appearance: Reflect on the true purpose of marriage, emphasizing the emotional experience over physical appearance. Consider that commitment, understanding, and love are essential emotions sought in a marriage,

challenging societal norms that prioritize physical attractiveness.

4. Life's Ultimate Purpose - Emotions: Grasp the idea that the ultimate purpose of life is solely emotions and feelings. Understand that, at the end of life, the memories carried forward and the essence of existence are rooted in emotional experiences, not material possessions or achievements.

5. Avoidance of Negative Emotions: Acknowledge the second emotional life purpose, which involves avoiding negative emotions like pain, fear, hatred, and insecurity. Realize that the quest for emotional well-being includes both seeking positive emotions and avoiding undesirable ones, shaping the overall purpose of life.

3. Key Takeaways for the Chapter - Sequencing The Want And Don't Want Feelings For A Purposeful Life

1. Emotions Define Life: Acknowledge that the purpose of life revolves around emotions. Whether

desiring certain emotions or avoiding others, emotions are the driving force behind our goals and decisions.

2. Emotional Priorities: Understand the importance of prioritizing emotions. Sequencing emotions reveals the true hierarchy of values, influencing decision-making and daily actions. Recognize that the order of emotions impacts the overall quality of life.

3. Personal Exercise: Engage in a self-discovery exercise to identify emotions you want to feel and those you want to avoid. Create two columns on a blank page, listing desired and undesired emotions. This exercise helps in understanding personal priorities.

4. Sequencing Significance: Emphasize the significance of correctly sequencing emotions. The order of importance influences behavior and decisions. Reflect on how prioritizing comfort over love, for instance, can shape one's actions and relationships.

5. Value Alignment: Grasp the importance of aligning personal values with desired emotions. Evaluate whether daily actions and decisions align with the prioritized emotions. Recognize that understanding and aligning values contribute to a more fulfilling and purposeful life.

4. Key Takeaways for the Chapter - Strategies For Recognizing Conflicts In Your Life Purpose

1. Recognize Emotion Conflicts: Understand the significance of checking for conflicts and sequences in emotions. Conflicting desires, such as wanting excitement but avoiding insecurity, can hinder personal growth.

2. Tug of War Analogy: Visualize internal conflicts as a tug of war between opposing emotions. The constant pull in different directions creates stress and hampers progress. Resolving conflicts involves aligning desired and undesired emotions.

3. Identify Conflicting Goals: Examine conflicting goals in various aspects of life. For instance, aspiring for fame but fearing judgment creates an internal struggle. Recognize that conflicting desires impede the achievement of goals.

4. Emotions Drive Goals: Acknowledge that goals are driven by emotions. Understanding the emotional motivations behind goals, such as the desire to feel special or admired, reveals the true purpose behind aspirations.

5. Correct Sequence and Resolve Conflicts: Emphasize the need to correct the sequence of emotions and resolve conflicts. Aligning the sequence with personal values and ensuring that 'want' and 'don't want' emotions complement each other enhances clarity and goal attainment.

5. Key Takeaways for the Chapter - Simplifying Life's Purpose: A Guide To Ease And Clarity

1. Conditions Shape Emotions: Realize that emotions, both positive and negative, are shaped by conditions. Examine whether these conditions are easy or hard, understanding that conditions influence how emotions are experienced.

2. Example of Relationship Conditions: Explore the impact of conditions on relationships. A couple's lack of love stemmed from unfulfilled conditions. Analyze personal relationships to identify and address conditions affecting emotional fulfillment.

3. Conditions for Feeling Rich: Consider the conditions set for feeling rich. Evaluate whether these conditions are attainable and realistic. Recognize that having excessively difficult conditions for positive emotions, like feeling rich, can lead to dissatisfaction.

4. Easy and Difficult Conditions: Distinguish between easy and difficult conditions for emotions. Understand that making conditions too hard for positive emotions and too easy for negative emotions can hinder happiness and fulfillment.

5. Simplify Conditions for Positivity: Simplify conditions for positive emotions. Learn from examples where individuals find happiness in simple, easily achievable conditions. Shift the focus from achieving grand goals to embracing readily attainable conditions for a more content and fulfilling life.

6. Key Takeaways for the Chapter - Crafting Empowering Emotional Conditions

1. Emotional Conditions Exercise: Engage in a transformative exercise to redefine the purpose of life. Create easy conditions for positive emotions and challenging conditions for negative emotions. This exercise enables a shift towards a fulfilling and

positive mindset, emphasizing the importance of emotional well-being.

2. Example of Financial Freedom: Illustrate the impact of easy and difficult conditions using the example of feeling financially free. Differentiate between setting challenging conditions, like achieving a specific income, and easily attainable conditions, such as affording daily luxuries like Pani Puri.

3. Goals vs. Emotional Conditions: Emphasize the distinction between setting ambitious life goals and establishing emotional conditions. Encourage setting lofty goals while ensuring emotional conditions are easily achievable, promoting a sense of contentment and positivity.

4. Affirmations for Easy Conditions: Provide examples of affirmations with easy conditions for positive emotions. Encourage participants to be creative in crafting affirmations tailored to their needs, fostering a positive mindset with readily achievable emotional conditions.

5. Emotional Resilience: Highlight the positive impact of the exercise on emotional resilience. By establishing easy conditions for positive emotions and challenging conditions for negativity, individuals become emotionally sturdy, better equipped to handle life's fluctuations without easily succumbing to negativity.

IN SEARCH OF MEANING: UNDERSTANDING LIFE'S ULTIMATE PURPOSE

"Embark on a profound journey to 'Discover Your Life Purpose,' where passion meets purpose, mindfulness becomes your guide, adversities are conquered, and everlasting happiness radiates from within."

This chapter is an extremely powerful chapter. This chapter is about the purpose of life. Can you tell what the purpose of your life is? What's your biggest purpose? What do you want to achieve in your life? Ask yourself, what is the biggest purpose you can think of before you die?

When the question is asked to people, they usually say that financial freedom is their purpose of life, some say serving people is their purpose, some say they want to transform lives, some wish for making a difference, some wants to help as many women as they can, some wants to spread happiness in the world, some people are dreaming of becoming a famous YouTube influencer. Some want to be a good human being, to build an ideal career, be a role model for their children, some just want to be happy, and some say that seeing God is the purpose of their life. Almost everyone has this type of purpose in their life.

But you wonder that 99% of people are wrong about the purpose of their life. The examples mentioned above cannot be the purpose of your life; these may be your goals. Most people confuse goals as the purpose of their life.

For example, you want to become a YouTube influencer. It's a goal. It's not the purpose of life. If you want to help as many women as you want. Is that a goal or is that a purpose? That is also a goal. It's not the purpose of life.

These cannot be the purpose because we can upgrade them. You can achieve a goal, you can achieve more goals, and after achieving one goal, your goal gets changed. So goals are different and purposes are different. Most people don't understand the meaning of purpose. People believe purpose is nothing but a goal that I want to discover. No, it's not a goal. What is a purpose? Let's understand for the first time the technical meaning of what really is the purpose of your life.

Purpose of life is only 'emotions', which is nothing but 'feelings', nothing else!! And if you don't believe me, I'll prove it to you right now. Think about it. Don't you want to have a big house for yourself one day? If you want to have a big house for yourself one day, you don't want a house. You want an emotion that comes out of that house. If there are four people who want a house. Do all four people want a house with the same emotion? No. Everybody has a different purpose. Everybody has an uncommon emotion. Some people want freedom from their own house. For some people, it means security. For some people, others it means relaxation. And for some, it is a feeling of having something of their own. For some, it's an achievement. For some, it is success. Bottom line is, you don't want a house, you want that emotion.

Humans are very emotional; we are not okay with it if we get the house without the emotion of security. Is it possible that you can achieve your house and you don't get that particular emotion which you are running behind? No! We are attached to emotions. You may have experienced this in your life. You achieve a particular goal that you've been waiting for five years, ten years in your life. The day you achieve that goal, suddenly you feel something is missing. I don't know why, I'm not feeling like something is missing. And you can't explain what is missing, but you feel something is missing. If you've experienced this in your life, you've achieved something after many, many years. And the day you achieve it, you don't feel satisfied. Something is missing. I'll tell you why. You got so obsessed with the goal that you forgot the purpose, which was the emotion. So because of which you got the house, but you didn't get the emotion. Because you completely forgot about the emotion, you completely forgot about the purpose of buying the house.

One more example, suppose you want to feel special. To feel special is an emotion. Now, does everybody in the world feel special? Is this the purpose of their life or is that the goal of their life? Yeah! That's a purpose, not a goal. That's a reason. The purpose means the reason. Purpose means the way you are doing this, the way behind the goal, the meaning behind the goal. The purpose behind the goal is the emotion. So feeling special is a purpose. But is it possible that some people will feel special simply if somebody says thank you to them? Is it possible? Yeah. But is it also possible that hundreds of people are becoming your fans and you may still not feel special? Is that possible? Yes! It's possible.

Unfortunately, most of the people have become obsessed with goals, not with purpose. The purpose of your life is always emotions. We only want an emotion out of every goal in life. Whether it is buying a house, whether it is buying a car, whether it is becoming an influencer, whether it is becoming successful, even helping other people. Is it okay if you felt nothing in the end? No, it's not. We need some feeling out of it; we do that for this feeling. This feeling can be as satisfaction or fulfillment or an emotion. But if that emotion is missing, what happens to that goal? That goal becomes empty. That goal becomes meaningless.

So what is the purpose? A purpose of life is only emotions and feelings, nothing else. What is called the experience of life's emotions? Nothing else. What is called quality of life? Emotions.

Chapter 2

TYPES OF EMOTIONAL PURPOSES

*"In the pursuit of 'Discover Your Life
Purpose,' witness the unfolding chapters
of passion, mindfulness, resilience, and
enduring happiness – a guidebook to a
life well-lived."*

There are two types of emotional purposes that we have. Two types of emotional reasons that we have been:

First Purpose:

First, you want to feel emotions in your life after achieving your goals. And these emotions are the reason you want to buy a house. You want to become a hope; you want to become a YouTube influencer. Why do you want to buy a car? Why do you want to make so much money in your life? You want to look good; you want a life partner. Achieving these gives us the feeling of happiness, security, satisfaction, joy, fun, self respect, love, care. All these are nothing but emotions. If something doesn't give you these feelings, are you okay with that? No!!

Now, let's take one more example. Suppose you buy a beautiful car. What is your dream car? Think about it. Is it a Mercedes? Is it an Audi? For me, it's a Rolls Royce. Now, whatever is your dream car, you're not behind a car. You're luxurious; behind the emotion that the car can give you. People who love Tesla are behind the emotion of technology and the automation of electric cars. One very common emotion why people want to buy a luxurious car is because they want to feel rich, they want to feel special; they want to show off, and they want others to look at them while they drive that car. Why? Because they want to feel special, they want to feel luxurious; they want to feel rich. These are called want feelings.

Whenever we are talking about getting married, most people are looking at marriage through looking at a person who's looking good first; they don't look at their good character. Why? Because if you're walking with a person who's beautiful, if you're walking with a person who's handsome, what happens? Society says, oh wow, what a wonderful couple they look. So the first criteria for everybody's attention are good looks. But if you're not actually looking for a handsome person, if you're not actually looking for a beautiful person. What are you looking for? What do you want? You want an emotion; you want commitment; you want understanding, and you want love. Is it okay if you get a handsome or beautiful partner but don't get commitment? Are you okay with that? No. So what is the purpose of marriage? Is it the beautiful person or is it the emotion that you get out of marriage? It's the emotion.

So remember, the purpose of life is always only and only emotions, nothing else. What do you die with? Do you die with a marriage? Do you die in a car? Do you die with a human being? No. You only die with one thing: your emotions. When you die that last minute, you will only remember your emotions. Do you know you can carry forward your emotions from one life to another life? We carry forward the memory of your emotions from one life to another. You may have heard about past life memories. When people have their past life memories, do they have memories of cars and bungalows? No. They have memories of their emotions. So that's the only purpose of your life.

Always remember that emotions and feelings are the only purpose of your life. Any big thing that you're talking about, a 100 crore company, a palace to live in or becoming the president of a country is a goal, not a purpose. Purpose is very simple; it is the emotional experience, nothing else.

Aren't you suddenly feeling very relaxed knowing the technical meaning that purpose is nothing but an emotion?

Second Purpose:

Second one is "I don't want to feel". Think about the emotions you are running away from? Do we all run away from the same emotion? Not necessarily. Some emotions are common between us. But not all emotions are common between us. We want to run away from the emotions like pain, fear, hatred, anger, loneliness, conflicts etc. Do you like conflicts? Of course, we don't like people fighting. So we don't want that emotion of conflict in our house. We don't want to feel insecure, sad, poverty. We don't want to feel poor. We don't want to feel rejected by other people. We don't want to feel anxiety in our life. We don't want to feel embarrassed, and we don't want to be embarrassed in front of ten people.

What we don't want to feel is also a purpose. The feeling of not wanting is equally important in the purpose of our life. For example, happiness is important, but not being depressed is also important. If I am rich, I'll feel insecure all the time. Do you want to be rich and insecure all the time? No. So what is important? Both feelings are important and both are the purpose of our life. We are constantly either running towards an emotion or we're running away from an emotion. This is the purpose of our life; these two things are the purpose of our life.

CHAPTER 3

SEQUENCING THE WANT AND DON'T WANT FEELINGS FOR A PURPOSEFUL LIFE

"Your life, a canvas waiting for purposeful strokes. 'Discover Your Life Purpose' and let your true passion, mindfulness, resilience, and unending joy paint the masterpiece of your existence."

From the previous chapter, we are clear about the purpose of our life. Can you recall what the purpose of your life is? Motorbike? Car? Harley Davidson? A beautiful person to marry? Spirituality? Finding God? No!! It's 'Emotions'. Which kind of emotions? I want to feel emotions and I don't want to feel emotions.

But the question is, when do these emotions get triggered in our life? When do we feel that 'we want to feel? When do we not feel that 'we don't want to feel? Check for sequence and conflicts first. What do I mean by that? Let's do an exercise.

Powerful Exercise:

Take a blank page like, and divine in two halves, creating two columns. The first column on the left side will say 'feel? I want to feel'. The second column will say 'I don't want to.'

I'll give you my example. Many years ago, when I did this exercise for the first time with my mentor, my 'want to' emotion was success. Let's randomly first write down what you want to feel? Do we all want to feel exactly the same emotions? No, not necessary. That is why our goals are different. Your goals are giving you your emotions, and my goals are giving me my emotions. Write down on your notepads your examples.

Let me share some examples for a better understanding. Your emotions can be like this: I wanted to feel success, I wanted to feel excited about life; I wanted to feel love in life; I wanted to feel comfortable in life, and I wanted to feel rich in life. And here are some 'don't want to' emotions: I did not want to feel a failure, I did not want to experience hard work, I did not want to work hard, I didn't want that experience of struggle in my life ever, I did not want to feel insecure, I did not want to feel conflicts, I did not like conflict, I used to always run away from conflicts, I never wanted to feel poor in my life.

Sequencing of Emotions:

But even though we've written what we 'want to feel' and what we 'don't want to feel', is the priority of these emotions in the correct sequence? Not necessarily. For example, do you think I wanted success at number one? When I wrote this list for the first time, you would say yes. Actually, no. I'll tell you my sequence. To be honest, comfort was my first priority, excitement was my second priority. Feeling successful was my third priority. Feeling rich was my fourth priority. And feeling love was my fifth priority. So if you observe very carefully, where has love gone? Low in the values. So if you look at this list and if you had met me those days, do you think I was successful in relationships those days? No. Because I wasn't valuing love. So was I vibrating at the frequency of love? No, I was not. But if you look at my list, I wanted comfort at number one. Can you tell me what my daily routine was? What time did I used to wake up? You can easily predict. Do you think I always woke up early in the morning or did I wake up late? Was I hardworking or was I lazy? I used to wake up at like 12:00 01:00 in those days and I was very lazy. I used to sit all the time, and I used to watch movies all the time. I wasn't fond of all this stuff, in those but I was doing these activities all day. What I wanted to feel all the time was the Comfort. I loved comfort in my life. So all my decision making came from comfort. So if I wanted to go to a family event and if that family event was required for me to go through an entire night journey, what do you think? I will say yes or no? I will say no. Because of my values, comfort was first.

I hope you are understanding the criticality of sequencing here. Now give sequence to the contents of your list. You don't need to be 100% accurate at this. Just implement as much as you understand. Forget about what you don't understand. Don't ask any questions to yourself, just give a sequence. You should be clear about having at least five emotions in life?

We all don't want to experience some kind of emotions in our life, but each emotion will have a certain value, will have a certain importance. So now go to your list of don't want feelings and give it a sequence. Sequence, what is the number one feeling that you don't want? What is the second feeling you don't want? What is the third feeling you don't want? What is the fourth feeling you don't want? What is the fifth feeling you do not want?

Does it mean that the first and the second have to be accurately first and second? No. Just make this exercise as per what you understand at this moment.

MAY I ASK YOU FOR A SMALL FAVOR?

I want to express my sincere gratitude for choosing to invest your time in reading this book. Your decision to explore this work among countless others means a lot to me.

I hope that within these pages, you've discovered actionable insights that can enhance your daily life. Your journey doesn't have to end here, though.

May I kindly request an additional 30 seconds of your valuable time?

Sharing your thoughts about the book through a review would be immensely appreciated. Your review serves as a beacon, guiding other readers to take a chance on my books. It's a small gesture that carries significant weight in the world of authors.

To submit your review effortlessly, please **Scan** the **QR Code** below. It will take you directly to the book's review page:

"Discover Your Life Purpose" or "Global Link"

Alternatively, you can also find the "**Reviews Section**" of this book's page on Amazon.

Your review will require just a minute of your time but will make a monumental difference in helping me connect with a broader audience and I eagerly look forward to reading your review.

Once again, thank you for your unwavering

CHAPTER 4

STRATEGIES FOR RECOGNIZING CONFLICTS IN YOUR LIFE PURPOSE

"Uncover the profound wisdom within you. 'Discover Your Life Purpose' – where passion is kindled, mindfulness prevails, adversities are triumphed, and happiness becomes an eternal flame."

Conflicts in Sequence

Now let's come to the main part along with the sequence. Check for sequence and check for conflicts. Here is an example of that: If I'm saying I want to feel comfortable and I don't want to feel like a failure, is this complementing or is this conflicting? It's complimentary. Let's look at the second one: I want excitement, but I don't want to be insecure in life. What gives you excitement in life? Something baffling, right? Like bungee jumping or a roller coaster ride or maybe finding new people in life and connecting to new people in life or starting new businesses. I want excitement, but I don't want insecurity. Are these matching or conflicting? It's conflicting. An excited person cannot feel insecure.

Let's take one more example. Let's say love is at my bottom. I want feelings of love, but I don't like conflicts. Are these complimenting or conflicting? It's a conflict. Do you want love also? And you don't want conflict as well. Are. If I want to be married without a single conflict in my life, it is next to impossible. It is not possible if two people stay together without having conflicts. Because of these conflicts, we are not attracting what we want in our life. There is a constant confusion in our life.

Do you remember the game we used to play in childhood called tug of war? So there used to be two teams in school. One team would stand on the other side, one team would stand on this side and we would hold a rope. You and your team would hold the rope from this side and the opposition team would hold the rope from another side and both are pulling towards their side. Who wins? The team pulled the other on their side. What if you are pulling on both sides? Who wins? Handshake your hands and start pulling both hands on their side. Pull right hand towards right and left hand towards left. Which hand is winning? No one. And who will get stressed? Only you. The same thing our internal conflicts do with us.

Everyone wants to make money. But ask yourself, why do you want to make money? What do you want to feel? Everyone and everybody have an unfamiliar emotion of why they want to make money. For some people, it is security. For some people, it is abundance, richness and luxury. Let's take an example. Say to yourself: "I want to feel rich." Now you're clear about what you want to feel, the moment you say 'I want to feel rich' the reason for becoming rich will be in your mind, now say "but I don't want to take risks". "I want to feel rich, but I don't want to take risks." Why? It's not the risk you're running away from. You're running away from a particular feeling. You may have thought about that feeling at the moment you said the affirmation. You know what you are running away from? Is this complementing or conflicting inside your emotions? Yes! Both your purposes are conflicting.

One more example: many people, mostly the youngsters, would love to become a YouTuber and would like to make money from YouTube videos. What emotion do people want by doing YouTube videos? Different people want different emotions. One of the common emotions is 'famous'. So let us say you're clear about what you want, say to yourself that "I want to be famous." Now say: "I want to be famous but I don't want to be judged." So your number one priority is 'I want to be famous.' Your number one 'don't' want emotion is 'I don't want to be judged.' Here is what will happen. You will open up your laptop, you'll try to make a video, and your mind will say, what if someone judges me? What if people don't like my video? What if nobody subscribes to my channel? That means people are judging me. I don't want that. Will you be able to make the video? Never! But you will get up in the morning and you will motivate yourself again. You know why? Because you want to be famous. Your thoughts are 'I want to be famous. I am going to make my video today' and you get all ready, all prepared. Start your laptop and what happens again: What if nobody likes my video? And there you go into a cycle again.

We all have experienced this internal conflict for many decisions in our life. Many times in many areas of life. You want to lose weight. You don't want to lose weight; you want an emotion. Losing weight is a goal. What is the emotion? What emotion do you want to feel by losing weight? No, you don't want to feel good; you don't want to feel fit, 90% of people want to look good, and they want to feel special. They want somebody to say, wow, you're looking good. They want that feeling of admiration. They want to impress people. Now I hope you are clear about what you want to feel. I want to feel special. I want to be admired. And you don't want to feel tired.

Will your affirmations work if there is an internal conflict? No! Therefore we need to solve this problem? So for the first time, here is what I want you to do. I want you to go and correct the sequence a little on your own. Check if you want love on the top. If love is your need, love should be at the top of the sequence. But if love is not on the top, maybe you should bring it on the top now. That should become the purpose of your life. Are you realizing you're struggling in your relationships? Yes? It is because love is not on the top right now. So bring it to the top. Change your sequence and resolve the conflicts. What do I mean by resolving the conflicts? See, if you're 'want emotions' and your 'don't want emotions' should be complementing. For example, you want to feel successful and you don't want to work hard, you don't want to struggle, will it complement? No, it'll be a conflict. So take some time and correct your sequence.

Let me show you my current want feelings which I created on my own for my purpose in life. When I get up in the morning, these are the emotions I want to feel. First emotion that I want to feel is love. I'm very clear about it. I'm very, very clear about it. This is my highest priority. What activity should I do in the morning to feel love? I hug my wife; I say I love you to her every morning. I play with my birds. I call up my mom; I call up my life, my family. Every morning, I call up my family members.

We should feel what we want to feel. I definitely want to feel successful, I definitely want to feel rich, and I also want to feel comfortable. So it's not like I don't want to feel comfortable. I want to feel comfort but at the end. Do you think failure should be in my number one position? No. But does it mean I should feel like a failure? No. So what I did was I took failure, and I said, no, I'm going to put it down. I made sure that I took conflicts, and I put them at the bottom. Conflict should always go at the bottom. So I don't want to feel like a poor person, I work hard for it. Love is my number one emotion and I don't want to feel poor. Is this conflicting right now? No. It's not conflicting right now because love and poverty have and nothing to do with each other. Is this making sense to you? Now you can realize that there are too many conflicts on your list.

There are so many conflicts because of which you're getting tired every day. You are thinking too much and hardly taking any action. The worst situation is for those people who have "artificial spirituality". They have the desire to make money, but they also have the 'don't' want a feeling of I don't want to feel materialistic in life. So they want to feel spiritual also and there's always a conflict. And then they don't get interested in working again.

Therefore, you should put effort in correcting your sequence, and you should try to resolve your conflicts. You have to decide what you 'want to' feel and what you 'don't want to' feel. What is the priority of 'not feeling'? And what is the priority of 'feeling'? Who can decide that for you? Only you. Imagine there is a plate in your hand and there are six items on the plate. Three items you want, three items you don't want. Who will decide which items you want? And which items you don't want to eat? Only you will decide. You're grown up, you have to decide. Even if I advise you to eat something of my choice, it will not work. Because you know when I will give you advice,

I will give you advice as per my purpose in life. And that is why my advice will always be wrong advice for you. So, me giving you advice will not help. So don't ask anyone if your 'want feeling' sequence is correct. Don't ask anyone if your 'don't want feeling' is correct.

But I can only show you a way to correct it later if you're going wrong. I can show you a method, but I can't correct it for you.

If you resolve these conflicts and if you take care of the sequence, you will be able to attract your goals in life.

CHAPTER 5

SIMPLIFYING LIFE'S PURPOSE: A GUIDE TO EASE AND CLARITY

*"Dive into the essence of your existence
with 'Discover Your Life Purpose.' A
transformative journey awaits – where
passion ignites, mindfulness guides,
adversities bow, and happiness becomes
the rhythm of your purposeful dance."*

Now we are clear about the purpose of our life and we are also clear about the sequence of our want feelings and the sequence of our 'don't' want feelings. And there is no conflict between the sequences. But the question is, whatever we've written, how do we really feel all of these emotions that we've written down? How do we fulfill this purpose of your life? Even though the sequence is correct, even though there's no conflict in life. Question is, how do we fulfill the purpose of our life? If we want to make a difference, how do we do that? Like if I want to feel successful, if I want to feel rich, if I want to feel love, the question is how will I feel these? We can do this by adding conditions.

Understanding Conditions

There are two types of conditions: easy conditions and hard conditions. All our emotions that we want to experience are experienced based on conditions. For example, many people love holidays in a chilly place and many people do not. life,Do people want to feel the same feeling from the holiday in similar conditions? No, we all have different conditions of holiday. Everyone wants to feel love in their life, but does everyone have the same conditions of love? No, everyone has different conditions of love. Everyone wants to feel successful in life, but everyone has different conditions. And there are always two types of conditions: there are easy conditions and there are hard conditions.

Everyone should say this affirmation: "we have very easy conditions", "we have very easy conditions" to experience the 'don't want' feelings. Yeah, you read it right, to experience the 'don't want' feelings. For example, you don't want to feel judged; you don't want to be judged. But you feel judged in a very, very easy condition. If somebody raises their voice with you, you feel like they're judging you. You're standing at a party and somebody is standing very far away from you and they're looking at you and they're just smiling. We have experienced this at a party and we feel very uncomfortable. What are they talking about? About you? You think they are talking about you and laughing at you, and you feel judged very easily. This means you have easy conditions for judgment. Which means you will feel judged easily even though you don't want that emotion. You have only created such judgments and conditions for yourself.

Here is another example: When you do business with someone, you have financial conditions. Like a financial agreement saying, we agree to this condition or that condition so that we can make so much profit. And when you make so much profit, you pay so much tax. We have government conditions about how many taxes we pay. Just like that, we have conditions for our emotions and we don't even realize that.

Example 1:

I'll give you an excellent example. There's a couple who came to me once for personal coaching and they were getting divorced. Their marriage was one year, and it was a love marriage. So this couple, when they came to me for the first time, I asked them, why do you want to be divorced? And the boy said, she doesn't love me. When I asked the girl, and she said he doesn't love me. So they both wanted a common emotion which they were not getting from each other. They're not getting love. And what did I say? Whether it is 'want' emotions, whether it is don't want emotions. We have conditions for these emotions, either we have easy conditions or we have hard conditions. So I asked this girl, I said, tell me, did you once upon a time feel like this guy loved you? She said, yeah, of course. We had a love marriage. I said, okay, so you don't feel love from him today? She said, no, he doesn't love me anymore. I said; tell me, why do you feel that? She said, I don't know,In those, but he doesn't love me. I said, no! You should think about it. What did he do once upon a time to make you feel love? What conditions did he fulfill for you to feel love? She said, I don't know. In those days, he used to call me every day from the office at least ten times. I was writing these notes when she was telling me all this. I said, very good. She was telling me all this. I said, very well. What else? Tell me more. How did he make you feel love initially in your relationship? She said, you know what? Every week, once or twice he used to give me a surprise, he used to bring me flowers, he used to bring me greeting cards, he used to take me to a beautiful restaurant, without even telling me. I said, okay. Then I asked her another question. I asked, is he fulfilling these conditions nowadays? She said, forget about one week. He hasn't given me a gift for the last six months. Gift for the last six months. I said, okay. Does he call you from the office every day? She said, no, he doesn't call me anymore, he's so busy in life all the time, he doesn't love me.

So do you see? She's not experiencing love because the conditions are not being fulfilled. Was this marriage going to last? No. Then I asked the boy. I said, tell me one thing. Why do you want to divorce her? He said: She doesn't love me. I said, okay. Why doesn't she love you? What do you mean by she doesn't love you? He said, you know what? Every time in my relationship, initially, whenever she made food, she used to always ask me what to make for you. Now she makes whatever she wants. She doesn't even ask me once in a day. She used to cook as per my choice before. I said, okay. What else did you like about when she loved you? And he said, she loved me and every day she used to have a romance with me. If I was holding her hands in the public, she would let me hold her hands. If I was giving her a hug, she would hug me back. I said, what happens now? He said, now she doesn't want to have romance. If I give her a hug, she says, hey, people are looking. What are you doing? If I hold her hands in public, she says, what are you doing? I said, okay, so she doesn't hold your hands, she doesn't give you a hug. For how long? He says, I don't remember the last time she gave me a hug. All the time, she has some excuse. So that means she's not fulfilling his conditions.

Now it's clear that relationships are made of conditions, emotions are made of conditions. These people don't love each other because they have hard conditions for marriage.

The boy had conditions that: She should ask me every day for food and should cook food only as per my choice. She should have a romance with me every time I want to have romance. Doesn't matter what her mood and state of mind is. She should say yes to everything I say. The girls also had similar conditions. She wanted him to call her daily from his workplace; she wanted to receive gifts twice or thrice a week. Is it easy or difficult? It became super difficult for both to fulfill each other's conditions.

We have made it very easy to feel negative. We have made it very difficult to feel positive.

Example 2:

Let's take one more example. There's this one guy who came to me and he said, Sooraj, I want to feel rich. I said, okay. Are you poor right now? He said, no, I'm not poor but I just want to feel rich. I said, what are you doing right now? This is not a young age boy I'm talking about. This is a senior gentleman. He said he's a vice president of his company, which is a bank. He's a vice president in a bank of a multinational company in India and if he does not feel rich, he does not feel successful. Isn't it crazy? You're the vice president of a bank and you're feeling like a failure. You don't feel successful; you don't feel rich. For him, feeling successful, feeling rich has hard conditions.

All our emotions have conditions. But his conditions are the hard conditions. He says, Sonora, until I don't have a bank asset of my own, until I don't have a company worth 100 core of my own, I'll never feel rich.

Is it good to have a big goal in life? Yeah, of course. You should have big goals. But the problem is his emotion has become difficult. Which emotion has become difficult? Emotion of being rich has become very difficult. He says he may not feel successful, he's not allowed to feel rich until he makes 100 crores. So what happens every day with him? He feels like a failure. Is there any use living a life like this? The purpose of this type of life is meaningless.

Example 3:

There's another person who says I want to feel special in my life. He's clear about what he wants to feel. He wants to feel special in his life. But to feel special, he says people have to see that I'm wearing Gucci, people have to see that I'm wearing Armani. Otherwise I won't feel special. So now he spends a lot of money on Armani, Gucci and everything. And the moment he has to wear anything else, he feels that he's not special. It's clear that he has difficult conditions.

We have very easy conditions for negative emotions. We have very difficult conditions for positive emotions. You are making a mistake if you have too many conditions. In fact, having too many conditions is also a problem. A person cannot be happy if he has too many conditions.

If you get angry easily in life, you have very easy conditions for anger. You come home and if somebody interrupts you while you're working; you get angry. You have very easy rules for feeling angry and irritated.

If you feel tired easily in the evening, you have very easy emotions for tiredness. Ten minutes of movement and you get tired. Another example, if you feel judged very easily if you feel disrespected very easily, if you get hurt very easily, if somebody disagrees with you and you feel judged, if somebody interrupts you when you're talking and you get upset, you have easy conditions for negative emotions.

We also have very difficult conditions for positive emotions. You have made your goals as your conditions to be happy, not your emotions. You should not make your goals as your conditions. I'll give you an example of my mentor who taught me this. He said, Sooraj, if I wake up in the morning and if I'm alive, I am happy. Is this an easy condition or a difficult condition? It's a super easy condition for him. If my life partner loves me by having a romance with me every day, then I have a happy married life. Is this an easy condition or a difficult condition? It's a very difficult condition. If my life partner is with me every day, she loves me. Is this an easy condition or a difficult condition? Super easy. She's with me every day. It's super easy. She can be with me every day.

Many people ask me, how do you have so much energy? Because I don't waste my energy, because I have very easy conditions for positive emotions and I have very difficult conditions for negative emotions. In my case, if someone has to hurt me, at least my entire family and at least 100 people have to come and say they don't like me. Then only I'm allowed to be hurt. Is this easy? My entire family comes and says I don't respect you. At least 100 people come and say I don't respect you on my face. Then only I'm allowed to feel disrespected and hurt. Is this an easy condition or a difficult condition? Super difficult.

There is this girl I know. About nine or ten months ago, she used to make Rs50,000 a month. This month she made ten lakhs. She calls me on the phone and she says, Sooraj Sir, life is tough for me. I naked her. What happened? She said, nothing is going right. She said, her income is down. I said, what do you mean? How much did you make this month? She said, I made only ten lakhs here. I said what? Why are you saying this? She said, last month I made 15 lakhs here. Even though she made 10 lakh, she is still feeling down because she made 15 last month. You'll see people like this in the stock market all the time. Even after this enormous achievements unsuccessful, she feels everything was wrong. Is it an easy condition to feel like a failure? Or is it a difficult condition to feel like a failure? Yes! It is a difficult condition. She thinks that every month her income has to be up.ago, If any month her income is even Rs1 less than last month and then she thinks she is unsuccessful. We are not aware of this, but we make our conditions difficult for us. That is why we feel frustrated. We have easy conditions for frustration. We easily get depressed because we have easy conditions for depression.

If you feel depressed, you are not actually depressed. You just have easy conditions for depression. Similarly, you're not feeling like a failure. You have easy conditions for failure. There can be somebody who's absolutely healthy and still feels bad about his body because they have easy conditions for feeling negative about their health. And there can be somebody who has cancer and still feels happy every day because they have easy conditions for positivity and difficult conditions for feeling bad.

My question to my readers is how do you want to die? Do you want to die with an easy purpose of life or a difficult purpose of life?

CHAPTER 6

CRAFTING EMPOWERING EMOTIONAL CONDITIONS

*"Unlock the secrets to a fulfilling life –
'Discover Your Life Purpose.' Embrace
your passions, cultivate mindfulness,
conquer adversities, and radiate the
everlasting glow of true happiness."*

I want you to perform an exercise right now-

For the first time in your life, get ready to recreate the purpose of your life with easy conditions for positive emotions and difficult conditions for negative emotions. I hope you will do this exercise right now. Take your notepads. You already know what you want to feel. You've done this exercise in the previous chapter. All I want you to do is now ask yourself in which conditions will you feel that feeling? I'll give you an example. If you want to feel rich every day, say this loudly to yourself: "when I will have five lakh rupees monthly passive income, only then I will feel rich and financially free". Is this an easy condition or a difficult condition? Super difficult, right? Okay, now let's do this again; repeat that even if I can afford Pani Puri every day, I am financially free. Is this an easy or difficult condition? It's super easy. This is how you can allow yourself to feel financially free. Does it mean you should not have a big goal? No. Of course, you should have big goals. In fact, you should make your goals big but make your emotional conditions easy. Make as many big goals as you want. But don't make your goals as your rules. Don't make your goals as your conditions. Make your emotional conditions very easy. Don't make them very difficult. In fact, make your negative emotional conditions very difficult.

Say, "Only when I exercise 1 hour every day, then I have a good willpower. Otherwise I don't have good willpower". Easy condition or difficult condition? Very difficult. You can change this into this: "Even if I exercise five minutes every day, I have an amazing willpower." You can easily do five minutes of exercise every day. What if you say like this- "I do perfect exercise for five minutes, perfectly without a single mistake, only then I'm good at my willpower." Is it easy or difficult? This again became difficult. "Even if I'm moving my hands for five minutes, I'm exercising and I have an amazing willpower." Easy or difficult? Very easy. Now you will say that by doing this, minutes, aren't we making life too easy? Yes, we are. But we are making positive emotions easy and negative emotions difficult. If you have easy and difficult negative emotions, what frequency will you vibrate at? Low, medium or high? Super high. And when you vibrate at high frequency, your emotions will attract amazing goals in your life. And sometimes, even if you don't attract your goals, will your frequency go down? No. Why? Because you have easy conditions for positive emotions. And you have difficult conditions for negative emotions.

Your life becomes beautiful when you finish this exercise. So do this exercise and be creative. Everyone has their own conditions based on their need and purpose. When you decide your conditions, you don't need to look for what the conditions of other people are. And you don't need anybody's approval on your conditions. You don't even need God's approval. Because God doesn't have time to approve of your conditions. Because God has not even created your conditions. Who created your conditions? You did. So why should God do the approval part? You did the work, so you will do the approval.

Now do one more affirmation. Put your hand on your heart and say I love you "your name", repeat this again and again. If I say I love you to myself. I have too much love in my life. Is this an easy or difficult condition for love? It's easy. If you say that "I will feel love when all my family members will love me", Easy or difficult? Super difficult. Some people are depressed because of these kinds of difficult rules in life. It's your life. Why will other people live by your game? You create your own conditions.

On your notepad, for each emotion I want you to write down easy emotions for the emotions that you want to feel. Invent easy conditions. Also, write down difficult conditions for the negative emotions in your life that you don't want to feel. If you don't want to feel hatred in your life, you can write- "I am allowed to feel hatred only when there is an earthquake in five countries at the same time." You will think that this is crazy, but that's the idea. Write impossible conditions for your negatives and write super easy conditions for your positives.

Some examples of affirmations:

- I feel happy when I eat food daily. It's easy.

- I feel excited and fun when I drink water. That is super easy.

- I'm successful if I wake up every day. It's easy.

- I will only feel angry when a hundred bulls will come and hit me. That is super difficult.

- I am loved when I'm with myself. It's easy.

- I am happy only if I have a normal life forever. It is super difficult.

- I feel happy when I walk in nature. It's easy.

- I feel rich even if I can afford to buy bread.

- Being able to watch my favorite episode means I have luxury.

If you do this exercise properly, you'll be like a mountain. Things won't shake you easily. Life will come, life will go, people will come, people will go, but they won't be able to shake you easily. If you have easy conditions for positive emotions and difficult conditions for negative emotions.

Make your own conditions. Play it like a game. You don't have to be perfect. You just have to create some conditions, that's it.

CONCLUSION

Congratulations on reaching the culmination of this book. Your commitment to reading through these pages signifies your dedication to personal growth and a thirst for knowledge. Completing a book is a remarkable achievement, and you should take a moment to acknowledge your accomplishment.

Throughout this journey, the aim has been to guide you toward shaping a destiny defined by success and fulfillment. Your investment in this book reflects a deep commitment to self-improvement, and for that, you should feel proud.

As you conclude this book, I trust that it has left you with valuable insights and a sense of empowerment. The road to a prosperous destiny is not always linear or without its challenges, but your newfound knowledge in smart questioning equips you to navigate these paths with confidence. I genuinely hope that your voyage through these chapters has been both enlightening and engaging. The pursuit of a splendid life brimming with happiness and fulfillment is a commendable one, and your proactive steps toward this aspiration are evident through your persistence in reading this book.

In the pursuit of success and a life well-lived, remember that knowledge is your most potent tool. With this, you hold the key to unlocking the limitless potential within you. As you close this final page and embark on the journey that follows, I extend my heartfelt best wishes for a future filled with accomplishments and contentment.

Cheers,

Sooraj Achar

MAY I ASK YOU FOR A SMALL FAVOR?

I want to express my sincere gratitude for choosing to invest your time in reading this book. Your decision to explore this work among countless others means a lot to me.

I hope that within these pages, you've discovered actionable insights that can enhance your daily life. Your journey doesn't have to end here, though.

May I kindly request an additional 30 seconds of your valuable time?

Sharing your thoughts about the book through a review would be immensely appreciated. Your review serves as a beacon, guiding other readers to take a chance on my books. It's a small gesture that carries significant weight in the world of authors.

To submit your review effortlessly, please **Scan** the **QR Code** below. It will take you directly to the book's review page:

"Discover Your Life Purpose" or "Global Link"

Alternatively, you can also find the "**Reviews Section**" of this book's page on Amazon.

Your review will require just a minute of your time but will make a monumental difference in helping me connect with a broader audience and I eagerly look forward to reading your review.

Once again, thank you for your unwavering

PREVIEW OF MY BEST SELLING BOOKS

Series-1: Master Your Life with NUMEROLOGY

★ **Why do 80% of People Fail to Recognize their True Potential ??**

These self-help books will help you **Recognize, Transform, and Navigate** your life toward a **Happier Destiny**.

I always say that your **Date of Birth** is so precious. God has placed many diamonds on your date of birth that you are not aware of. It doesn't matter if your date of birth is good or bad. The idea is how you can take the best out of your date of birth.

Master Your DESTINY With Numerology is a perfect, **complete beginner's guide** for those who are new to numerology.

★ What Role Does Numerology Play in Your Life?

- You have been surrounded by numbers since the day you were Born. Now use them to unlock your Destiny.

- Wherever you go in your life, the numbers always move on with you.

- When you are born, on the very first day of your life, you get your date of birth, which is made up of numbers.

- When you get admitted to school, you get your roll number.

- When you get your results, you get a percentage of numbers.

- When you get a job, you get a salary and EMP-ID number.

- When you buy any vehicle, it has a number plate.

- When you travel, you get a ticket and seat number

- When you check into a hotel, you get a room number.

- When you want to call a person, you have to dial numbers.

- When you get married, there is also a date attached to it.

- If there is Life, there are Numbers. You cannot get rid of Numbers.

★ Your **Name Spelling** also plays an important role according to your date of birth. Believe me or not, **30% to 40%** of your success or failure depends on your name spelling. If you keep your name spelling correct, you can achieve 30% to 40% more success in your life.

♥ Master Your DESTINY With Numerology will help you...

✓ Recognize Your Strengths and Weaknesses.

✓ Find Your Lucky Numbers and Colors.

✓ Correct Your Name Spelling without changing your documents.

✓ Choose the Right Profession.

✓ Find a Compatible Life-Partner.

✓ With Simple Remedies for All Your Problems.

✓ Check Your Foreign or Abroad Opportunities.

✓ Predict your Future Years, Months, and Days of importance, which helps you make Better Decisions.

✓ Understand the Behavioral Patterns of People Around You.

✓ Transform and Navigate your life for a Better Future.

★ If you are ready to make a commitment to yourself that you want to learn everything that is presented to you, then it is our commitment to you that this will surely help you a lot. There is no reason why this book will not change your destiny or transform your future. But, there is an important thing you must keep in mind, i.e., **"You will bring this change through TRANSFORMATION, not through MIRACLES"**.

★ If you learn **Numerology**, then

(a) "You will be **awakened**", which makes it likely to "**transform**" your life.

(b) Ultimately, "You will be able to **navigate** your life".

★ Life is all about **"Awakening,"**, "**Transformation**," and eventually, "Knowing How To **Navigate** It?"

★ Order **Master Your DESTINY With Numerology** now to make the most of your

Health, Relationships, Career, and Money by unlocking the **Power of Numbers**.

<u>Check Out My Best Selling Books Here:</u>

1. Master Your DESTINY With Numerology

2. Master Your NAME-SPELLING With Numerology

3. Master Your RELATIONSHIPS With Numerology

4. Master Your MONEY With Numerology

5. Master Your HEALTH With Numerology

6. Master Your PROFESSIONAL GOALS With Numerology

Series-2: <u>Master Your Life with VASTU</u>

★ How Can These Books Work Miracles in Your Life?

This Self-Help Book is A Perfect Blueprint Describing Ancient Principles for Modern Living. A Step-by-step Practical Guide for Beginners to Creating a Positive Living Space and for Optimal Well-Being.

Learn:

★ How to Implement Feng-Shui/Vastu in your Day-to-Day Life !!

★ What Role Do Feng-Shui and Vastu Play in Your Life?

★ Relationship between Vastu and Feng-Shui?

Vastu is used to Diagnose, and Feng Shui is the Remedy. Vastu is used to identify the disease, and Feng Shui is the medicine. Vastu and Feng Shui are complementary to each other.

Vastu Shastra is an Ancient Indian Science of architecture and construction, which is based on the principles of harmony and balance between humans and their environment. The main focus of Vastu is to create a harmonious balance between the 5-Elements of nature, i.e., Earth, Water, Air, Fire, & Space. It emphasizes directions and orientation and uses various elements like colors, shapes, and materials to create a balance and positive energy in the living spaces.

Feng Shui, on the other hand, is a Chinese Philosophical System of harmonizing everyone with the surrounding environment. It is based on the principles of Qi (Chi), the life force that flows through all living things, and Yin and Yang, the balance of opposite forces. Feng Shui focuses on the placement of objects, furniture, and structures in living spaces to optimize the flow of energy, or "Qi." It also considers the orientation of the building, the placement of doors and windows, and the use of colors, shapes, & materials to create balance & harmony.

In summary, both Vastu and Feng Shui aim to create balance and harmony in living spaces, but Vastu is more focused on directions and orientation, while Feng Shui emphasizes the flow of energy & balance of opposing forces.

★ The Benefits of Reading This Book Include:

✓ **Health and Well-Being:** Vastu principles aim to create a harmonious and balanced environment that can promote physical, mental, and emotional well-being.

✓ **Financial Prosperity:** Vastu principles are believed to help attract positive energy and good fortune, leading to financial prosperity.

✓ **Improved Relationships:** Vastu principles can help create an atmosphere of peace and harmony, which can lead to improved relationships with family, friends, & colleagues.

✓ **Increased Productivity:** A Vastu-compliant environment is said to be conducive to productivity and efficiency, leading to greater success in personal & professional life.

✓ **Spiritual Growth:** Vastu principles are based on ancient Vedic knowledge and aim to promote spiritual growth & enlightenment.

✓ **Enhanced Creativity:** Vastu principles are believed to enhance creativity and inspiration, which can be beneficial for artists, writers, & other creative professionals.

✓ **Better Sleep Quality:** Vastu principles can help create a peaceful and relaxing environment, which can improve the quality of sleep and help reduce stress & anxiety.

✓ **Improved Mental Clarity:** A Vastu-compliant environment is said to help clear the mind and improve mental clarity, which can be beneficial for decision-making & problem-solving.

✓ **Enhanced Career Prospects:** Vastu principles can help align one's career goals with their personal strengths and abilities, leading to greater career success & satisfaction.

★ Overall, the benefits of Vastu can contribute to a more Balanced, Harmonious, & Fulfilling Life.

★ Order "Master Your DESTINY With Vastu" now to make the most of your Health, Relationships, Career, & Money by unlocking the Power of Directions.

Check Out My Best Selling Books Here:

1. Master Your DESTINY With Vastu

2. Master Your GROWTH With Vastu

3. Master Your
WEALTH With Vastu

4. Master Your
CAREER With Vastu

<u>Series-3</u>: <u>The Ultimate Self-Healing Mastery</u>

Embark on a transformative expedition with 'The Ultimate Self-Healing Mastery,' a soul-stirring collection designed to illuminate the path to self-discovery, healing, and fearlessness. Each book is a profound exploration of fundamental aspects of human existence, guiding readers toward a purposeful, holistic, and fearless life.

1. Discover Your Life Purpose: Reveal Your True Calling

Uncover the secrets to a fulfilling life in 'Discover Your Life Purpose.' Illuminating the essence of your being, this book takes you on a profound journey to reveal your true calling. Master the art of purposeful living, radiate enduring joy, and align your actions with your life's deeper meaning. Through insightful practices and wisdom, you'll embark on a transformative odyssey to live a life that resonates with authenticity.

Key Themes: Life Purpose, Joyful Living, Authenticity

2. The Alchemy of Healing: Master Ancient Hawaiian Technique

In 'The Alchemy of Healing,' delve into the ancient Hawaiian wisdom that transcends time. Crush negative emotions, unravel subconscious patterns, and embark on a journey of self-healing for a holistic lifestyle. This book is a guide to harnessing the power within, using age-old techniques to restore balance, foster well-being, and tap into the alchemy that transforms challenges into opportunities for growth.

Key Themes: Ancient Healing, Emotional Wellness, Self-Healing

3. The Fear of Death: Conquer Mortality Anxiety, Live a Fearless Life

Confront the universal fear in 'The Fear of Death.' Recognize the human fears surrounding mortality, and transcend anxiety by embracing death as a natural part of life's journey. This book provides profound insights into conquering fears, living fearlessly, and understanding the deeper spiritual dimensions of existence. Gain wisdom to navigate life with courage, appreciating the transient nature of our earthly sojourn.

Key Themes: Fearlessness, Death Acceptance, Spiritual Wisdom

The Unifying Thread:

Each book in 'The Ultimate Self-Healing Mastery' is a standalone guide, yet together they form a cohesive narrative of personal growth, healing, and spiritual enlightenment. Authored by experts in their respective fields, these volumes offer a holistic approach to living—a roadmap to self-realization, emotional well-being, and a fearless embrace of life's profound mysteries.

Why Read the Trilogy?

Holistic Transformation: Embark on a journey that addresses the core aspects of your existence—purpose, healing, and fearlessness.

Expert Guidance: Benefit from the insights of experts who blend ancient wisdom with modern understanding to guide you toward a more meaningful and joyful life.

Practical Wisdom: Each book is a practical guide, filled with exercises, techniques, and profound teachings that can be applied in daily life.

Life-Altering Perspectives: Gain transformative perspectives on life purpose, healing practices, and the fear of death, allowing you to navigate challenges with resilience and grace.

Experience the synergy of purpose, healing, and fearlessness—the essence of 'The Ultimate Self-Healing Mastery.' This series is not just a collection of books; it's a transformative odyssey inviting you to explore the depths of your being and awaken to the infinite possibilities that life unfolds.

<u>Check Out My Best Selling Books Here:</u>

 1. Discover Your Life Purpose

 2. The Alchemy Of Healing

 3. The Fear of Death

<u>Series-4: Energize Your Mind, Body & Soul</u>

Embark on a transformative journey of self-discovery, inner balance, and empowered living with the 'Energize Your Life Trilogy.' This compelling series unveils profound insights and practical wisdom to help you attain holistic well-being, align with your life's purpose, and cultivate the energy needed for a harmonious and fulfilling existence.

1. The Art of Balancing YIN-YANG Energy: Discover the Secret to Energized Living

Uncover the ancient wisdom of balancing YIN-YANG energy in 'The Art of Balancing YIN-YANG Energy.' This book is your guide to attaining wholeness, finding inner equilibrium, and experiencing serenity in your everyday existence. Learn the secrets of Chinese philosophy and energy balance to lead an energized life filled with vitality and peace. Discover practices to harmonize opposing forces, fostering a sense of completeness and tranquility.

Key Themes: Energy Balance, Wholeness, Serenity

2. The 7 Energy Needs: Discover the 7 Keys to Personal Fulfillment

In 'The 7 Energy Needs,' explore the keys to personal fulfillment and emotional well-being. Align your needs with your goals, master the art of balancing vital energies, and unlock the secrets to a harmonious life. This book provides a comprehensive framework for understanding and fulfilling your core energy needs, empowering you to lead a life rich in purpose, joy, and fulfillment.

Key Themes: Personal Fulfillment, Emotional Well-Being, Harmonious Life

3. The Power of ONE QUESTION: Master the Art of Smart Questioning

Ignite your journey to greatness with 'The Power of ONE QUESTION.' This book is a game-changer, offering insights into the art of smart questioning. Revolutionize your thinking, enhance decision-making, and supercharge your life and career by asking the right questions. Uncover the transformative power of focused inquiry and learn to navigate life's complexities with clarity, purpose, and a profound sense of direction.

Key Themes: Smart Questioning, Decision-Making, Journey to Greatness

The Unifying Thread:

The 'Energize Your Mind, Soul & Body' seamlessly weaves together the threads of ancient wisdom, modern psychology, and practical strategies. Each book stands as a beacon, guiding readers toward a more balanced, purposeful, and empowered life. The trilogy is designed to be both a comprehensive roadmap and a practical toolkit for individuals seeking a holistic approach to well-being and personal development.

Why Read the Trilogy?

1. **Holistic Well-Being:** Dive into a series that addresses the various dimensions of your well-being, from energy balance and emotional fulfillment to smart questioning and decision-making.

2. **Practical Wisdom:** Each book is crafted with practical exercises, actionable insights, and transformative practices that can be integrated into your daily life.

3. **Personal Empowerment:** Gain the tools and knowledge needed to take charge of your energy, align with your purpose, and make informed decisions that propel you toward greatness.

4. **Ancient Wisdom, Modern Application:**

Discover the timeless principles of ancient philosophies and see how they can be applied in the context of contemporary living.

Embark on a journey of self-mastery, inner harmony, and empowered living with the '**Energize Your Mind, Body & Soul**.' Let this series be your guide as you explore the depths of your potential and unlock the secrets to a more vibrant, purposeful, and harmonious life.

<u>Check Out My Best Selling Books Here:</u>

1. The Art of Balancing YIN-YANG Energy

2. The 7 Energy Needs

3. The Power Of ONE Question

Series-5: LIFE-MASTERY Bundle

From Book 1: **"Master Your DESTINY & NAME-SPELLING With Numerology"** takes you on an enlightening journey into the mystical world of numerology, where the power of numbers shapes the fabric of our destiny. In this comprehensive guide, author Sooraj Achar unravels the secrets behind the numbers that influence your life, offering profound insights into the science of numerology.

In This Book, You'll Discover:

1. Unlock Your Destiny: Explore the ancient science of numerology and unravel the mysteries of numbers that shape your life.

2. Name Spelling Mastery: Delve into the

profound impact of name spelling on your destiny, discovering the hidden meanings within the letters.

3. Numerology Basics: Understand the core principles of numerology, from birthdate analysis to decoding the vibrations in your name.

4. Transformative Power: Witness real-life examples showcasing the significant shifts that occur when altering the arrangement of letters in your name.

5. Personal Year Number Insights: Navigate the various phases of your life with wisdom by understanding the influence of your Personal Year Number.

6. Destiny Number Revelation: Calculate your Destiny Number to gain insights into your life's purpose, talents, and challenges, empowering informed decision-making.

7. Practical Tools: Engage in practical

exercises, guided meditations, and interactive worksheets to apply numerology to your daily life.

8. Holistic Empowerment: Combine ancient wisdom with modern insights to create a holistic guide that empowers you to take charge of your destiny.

9. Transformative Journey: Whether you're a beginner or an experienced practitioner, embark on a journey of self-discovery, empowerment, and manifesting your fullest potential.

10. Illuminate Your Path: Decode the mysteries surrounding your name and birthdate, mastering your destiny through the profound wisdom of numerology.

11. Your Journey Begins Now: "Master Your DESTINY & NAME-SPELLING With Numerology" is your transformative tool for self-discovery and empowerment. Take

the first step towards unlocking the secrets of your destiny.

1. Master Your DESTINY & NAME-SPELLING With Numerology

2. Master Your HEALTH & RELATIONSHIPS With Numerology

TESTIMONIALS

These are a few feedbacks from my clients across different parts of the world. Kindly go through their reviews to understand how Numerology and Vastu helped them.

1. Ekta Gupta – Kolkata, India

"2021 is a difficult year for me. I have consulted a few numerologists. I have received vague answers and complicated solutions. I'm new to numerology. Charges were expensive. Sooraj is a good and kind soul. He is very patient with me. He answered all my questions. I had 1000 questions. More ever he helped me

to find a business name with no extra charges. I'm grateful to him. With your help, I'm sorted out with my business name. I had a lot of anxiety about it. I'm confident now. Sooraj is a helpful soul. He is patient and explains if one has questions. He doesn't rush into closing the job. You can consult him easily. I am going to recommend him to newbies like me. He is not going to cheat you or misguide you".

2. Neetu Ganglani - Stanley, Hongkong

"Hello Sooraj, I can't thank you enough. At the age of 45, I could find an ideal life partner for myself. And my compatibility with the boy I like. Got to know our strengths and weaknesses. Your suggestions helped me to find the right life partner. You have a bright future. Good luck"

3. R Lensly Kwaimani - Solomon Islands, Oceania

"Dear friend, glad I came across you. My daughter Felinda Kwaimani is sick for a long time and I was very much worried. Thank you for giving suggestions and guidance".

4. Seham Shabhir - Talagang, Pakistan

"You're one of the best numerologists...your predictions are correct...you are a very humble person...you gave answers to all of my questions in detail ... I'm very thankful to you. Ur remedies prove very helpful for me. He is the very best numerologist... I recommend him for all.. u should consult him to get rid of your problems..his remedies work like a magic"

5. Naveen Kumar - Bengaluru, India

"Sooraj is a gem as a human and as a professional. Before approaching Sooraj, I have enquired and got inputs from other numerologists and I did some research as well. I Was not satisfied with the answers provided by them and most of them were behind fees, even after paying for the consultation they charge extra for clarifying doubts. However, Sooraj was awesome in client satisfaction and the way he follows up with the client for providing suggestions. He takes the initiative to follow up and provide the best solutions and describes the reason for the input. I definitely suggest Sooraj to anyone who is looking for start-up business names or anything related to numerology. He has a good amount of knowledge and patience to answer all my queries".

6. Sneha S - Karnataka, India

"Hi Sooraj, it's a great prediction starting from Personality Traits to our Abroad Opportunities to future achievements. Everything is perfectly predicted with correct proof and explanations which help us to understand our lives better and take steps accordingly to numerology. Everyone are curious to know more about their life just to know when, how & what situations they will come across and how they need to overcome everything. Thanks a lot, Sooraj, for the best Numerology Prediction which helped us to understand ourselves better".

7. Aditya S - Mumbai, India

"Sooraj, your numerology predictions are brilliant and accurate. Your Suggestions

helped me find out whether my current job is suitable for me or not. I would suggest people consult you in due course of time".

8. M Nabanita - West Bengal, India

"Hi Sooraj, it's helpful and gives me a quick idea and help. Thank you so much for being there. It helped me to understand my situation It helps in my career and marriage. The information is good".

9. N Naresh – Bangalore, India

"Hello Sooraj, it was satisfactory. Can decide further based on the info shared & also can see positive outcomes looking forward to checking how it works".

10. Harishchandra Dnyaneshwar Deshmukh – Delhi, India

"Hi sir, Padhai puri nahi kar paya, 11 k salary he, Stable nahi hu life me, Business success nahi milta. Thank u sir for sharing my report and helping me understand my strengths and weaknesses".

AUTHOR PROFILE

Follow **the Author's Profile Page** to get updates on all his books: **https://amazon.com/author/sooraj_achar**

Grab your **Free Gift** if you missed it: **https://gift.sooraj-achar.com/**

Please Leave Your **Valuable Review** here: **"The Power of One Question"**

For 1-to-1 consultation, scan the **QR code** or contact: **connect@sooraj-achar.com**

Follow the **Author's BookBub** Profile:

https://www.bookbub.com/authors/sooraj-achar

Stay Connected to the **Author's Social Media Handles** below:

https://amzn.to/3CgQHF9

https://medium.com/@soorajachar99

https://bit.ly/3M7gIu2

instagram.com/psychology_of_numberz/

https://bit.ly/3dO6aDh

https://bit.ly/3LXBTyz

https://bit.ly/3E9vKxc

DISCLAIMER

This book is for educational purposes only. Readers acknowledge that the author does not render legal, financial, medical, or professional advice. The content within this book has been derived from various sources. Please consult a licensed professional before attempting any techniques outlined in this book.

By reading this document, the reader agrees that under no circumstances is the author responsible for any direct or indirect losses incurred as a result of the use of the information contained within this document, including but not limited to errors, omissions, or inaccuracies.

Adherence to all applicable laws and regulations, including international, federal, state, and local governing professional licensing, business practices, advertising, and all other jurisdictions, is the sole responsibility of the purchaser or reader.

Neither the author nor the publisher assumes any responsibility or liability whatsoever on behalf of the purchaser or reader of these materials. Any perceived slight of any individual or organization is purely unintentional.